DEVOTIONAL

WITH US

Awaken Ministries International welcomes you to your 21-day journey of hope and courage! The devotional, based upon the powerful anthem "You Are With Us," uses the lyrics of the song as a guide. Scott Ingegneri, Founder, and President of Awaken Ministries International is the co-writer of the song together with his wife, Lydia Ingegneri, and also Michael Farren, and Benji Cowart.

Scott developed the concepts of this project to awaken the hearts of readers to kingdom realities and biblical truth. Each day includes a line from the song, a scripture, a short spiritual message, and a prayer. As you engage with the Lord through the song, we hope that you recognize that you are not alone in this world and that you have an ever-present God who daily empowers His children to walk in courage.

Blessings,

The Awaken Ministries Team

AWAKENMINISTRIES.CO

YOU ARE WITH US

Awaken Ministries International 21 Day Devotional

Devotional Written by Scott Ingegneri

Song Written by: Benji Cowart, Lydia Ingegneri, Scott Ingegneri, Michael Farren

© 2018 Awaken Ministries International

For permissions contact:
contact@awakenminsitries.co

ISBN-13: 978-1725930971

YOU ARE WITH US

Written by: Benji Cowart, Lydia Ingegneri, Scott Ingegneri, Michael Farren

VERSE 1
Your kingdom is here
Your kingdom is now
Oh, we will not wait
We will not back down

VERSE 2
You lead us with light
And darkness must bow
For You are our strength
And the reason we can shout

CHORUS
You are with us, God Almighty
We are Yours, we will not fear
Ever forward, love's our banner
You are with us
You are with us!

VERSE 3
We stand on Your Word
And strongholds come down
As we move where You lead
Let Your presence shake the ground!

BRIDGE
And the gates, of hell, shall not prevail
You are life, You are truth, our Emmanuel
At the end, of it all, when our race is run
We will give, You the crowns, You've already won

*"The kingdom of God does not come with observation; nor will they say,
'See here!' or 'See there!' For indeed, the kingdom of God is within you."*
Luke 17:20-21 (NKJV)

As a father of four children I have experienced many father-to-child moments. I remember a specific evening that my family and I were on a walk. There was a path that was very dark and the kids were afraid to go that direction. I asked them if the dark was still scary to them if I was present. They decided that darkness was only scary to them if they were alone, therefore leading to the conclusion that darkness is not so scary. Being alone is what's scary.

The Kingdom of God is within you. What an amazing realization! Whenever we are faced with anything that has the appearance of darkness or the unknown, what is there to fear? We are not alone!

This reality caused my children to walk, laugh, dance, and skip down a dark pathway. At one point I actually had to pull my kids back a little bit because they were so confident and had run too far ahead of me!

As children of God, we walk and live with the reality of Heaven being within us. We can have the confidence to move forward despite any unknowns.

PRAYER: Father open my eyes to the reality of Your present Kingdom within me and around me. I repent of fear and ask You to help me walk in confidence, fully trusting You. Help me to see earthly things through the lens of Kingdom realities. I put ALL of my trust and my faith in You. Let's walk!

"For he has rescued us from the dominion of darkness and brought us into the kingdom of the Son he loves, in whom we have redemption, the forgiveness of sins."
Colossians 1:13-14 (NKJV)

The Kingdom of God is the essence of the Church's message and life. We are called to the Kingdom's life and power in the present, while still anticipating its final fullness and consummation in the future.

If you're a parent you have undoubtedly been asked this question countless times, "are we there yet?" As you read those words just now, were you envisioning your child asking that question with the typical whiny voice, exasperated tone, and over exaggerated body language? Wait. Maybe that's just me! The truth is, every child asks this question! I will add that not every time is the question accompanied by whining and complaining. Kids also ask this question out of genuine sincerity of simply wanting to know, "are we there yet?" Others, well, their goal is to annoy mom and dad!

There is an innate curiosity in all of us to know if we have arrived at our destination.

The amazing reality is that we have Kingdom fulfillment to look forward to, but we also have the present nature of the Kingdom to enjoy and walk in. There is joyful expectation of the future in Christ, but there is also a joyful reality of the present nature of His Kingdom. Israel had only the expectation of that which was to come.

"And you shall be to Me a kingdom of priests and a holy nation."
Exodus 19:6 (NKJV)

In Exodus 19:5-7 the Lord indicates His objective for His delivered people. He had a redemptive purpose for them with a priority of

Kingdom reinstatement. The deliverance of Israel from Egypt was God revealing His plan for the Church to be delivered and to walk in Kingdom dominion.

> *"Now all these things happened to them as examples, and they were written for our admonition, upon whom the ends of the ages have come."*
> *1 Corinthians 10:11 (NKJV)*

We have a present reality of His Kingdom. We get to live in the reinstated Kingdom state. Wow! What an amazing reality that the Kingdom of God is now!

PRAYER: Thank you Father for delivering me from darkness into the Kingdom of light. My heart's desire is to walk in the dominion that You reinstated for me to function from and live in. Thank you for what is to come, and thank you for that which is now!

"But without faith it is impossible to please Him, for he who comes to God must believe that He is, and that He is a rewarder of those who diligently seek Him." Hebrews 11:6 (NKJV)

The understanding that the Kingdom of God is now, and not just something to look forward to in the future, causes a current reality response. It moves us from simply waiting around for Heaven to eventually come, to joining God in the transforming power and work of His Kingdom now.

As I look through the stories in God's Word, even the greatest men and women of faith were given a role in the story that God was orchestrating in their lives. Faith always moves us into action. Abraham, Moses, Joshua, Jonah, Nehemiah, Peter, Paul, and so many others had to go, obey, and open their mouths.

We are called to live courageously and to put action to our faith. You may say, "I'm afraid!" The best way to break fear is to act. It is one thing to pray about a situation. It's another thing to do something about it.

There is an amazing story in the book of Mark. It's a story of a paralyzed man who convinced his four friends to take him to Jesus. The friends were probably exhausted and slightly annoyed from carrying him across town to where Jesus was, but the man was determined. When they got there it was too crowded and they couldn't get in. I can just picture the man telling his friends, "we are not going home until I get my miracle!"

This paralyzed man understood that you are closest to your victory when you face the greatest opposition. A lot of people would have stopped upon seeing the large crowds. They would have given up and returned to their homes defeated and believing the lie that it wasn't

the Lords will to heal them. This story has caused me to often say, "if you can't get through the door, go through the roof."

The paralyzed man did not allow the crowds or any opposition stop him from getting to Jesus. He commanded his friends to take him up to the roof, break through the roof, and lower him down to Jesus! This right here my friends, is faith in action. Jesus was in the middle of His sermon as dust and debris begins to fall. Suddenly, the roof busts open and men appear. As soon as there's a big enough opening for the paralyzed man to fit through, they lower him down right in front of Jesus.

> *"When Jesus saw their faith, He said to the paralytic,*
> *"Son, your sins are forgiven you." Mark 2:5 (NKJV)*

Do you have a faith that God can see? This story tells us that Jesus saw past this mans heart. Jesus saw his action. Faith is not the result of effort, but surrender. It is the fruit of God's work in us.

PRAYER: Thank you Father for delivering me from darkness into the Kingdom of light. My heart's desire is to walk in the dominion that You reinstated for me to function from and live in. Thank you for what is to come, and thank you for that which is now!

"You will be betrayed even by parents, brothers and sisters, relatives and friends, and they will put some of you to death." Luke 21:16

Apparently Jesus was never taught how to give a pep talk! This scripture in Luke does not seem to be what I would picture as the most encouraging pep talk of all time. Yet with staggering promises of everlasting joy, Jesus unleashed a movement of radical, loving risk-takers!

Christ calls us to take risks for kingdom purposes. Almost every message of American consumerism says the opposite. The world system convinces us to maximize comfort and security right now, not in heaven. Christ does not join that chorus. Our call is less the sprint, more the marathon.

In the popular movie "Braveheart" there is a famous scene where William Wallace (portrayed by Mel Gibson) and his army are facing a sea of warriors staring them down. Williams Wallace says, "Aye, fight and you may die. Run, and you'll live, at least a while. And dying in your beds, many years from now, would you be willin' to trade ALL the days, from this day to that, for one chance, just one chance, to come back here and tell our enemies that they may take our lives, but they'll never take...OUR FREEDOM!"

This amazing speech from William Wallace shakes his outnumbered army awake. William and his men face the enemy head on.

As Christians we have a promise of victory. God says in His word that the enemy has been defeated and will not prevail against the Kingdom of Heaven. Even so, believers still back down from the battle though victory has already been accomplished! William Wallace and his warriors did not have a promise of victory, still they fought with all their might.

We have a real reason to not back down. We have a risen Jesus who promises to build His church and that the gates of hell will not prevail against it. This is the very reason why we as believers can stand boldly and unwavering against forces of darkness.

It should be no surprise that Christ in us would lead us to take a stand and not back down. Jesus himself didn't back down before Pharisees, Sadducees, and all his accusers. The apostles didn't back down when it seemed all were against them.

PRAYER: I choose today to not back down. Fear will not be my guide. I will not allow circumstances or the uncertainties of this world to cause me to be hindered. I choose to STAND and take my place as a mighty warrior in the Kingdom of God!

"When Jesus spoke again to the people, he said, "I am the light of the world. Whoever follows me will never walk in darkness, but will have the light of life." John 8:12 (NKJV)

Notice that when you follow Him you also have Him. What a promise! "I am the light of the world. Whoever follows me. . . will have the light."

Jesus is saying that if you follow Him, you will have Him! He is making Himself fully available to us. All of Him becomes available to us. He is our Shepherd, our Sacrifice, our Living Water, our Bread from Heaven, our God, and our Light!

I remember a camping trip years ago where the power of light became very clear to me. It was a cloudy night no light was visible from the moon or stars. Being a city boy who is used to always having a glow of light, this wasn't something I was used to. As a match was lit to light up the campfire, it amazed me how the shine of a small match could be seen from such a distance. A small light stands above great darkness. How much more the greatest light of all, Jesus Christ?

Walking in the light is the opposite of walking in darkness. It means seeing reality for what it is. When you realize the power of light, and the power of God as your light, the path doesn't seem so difficult to find. You simply need to look up enough to follow the light. Being led by His light means that God becomes your overwhelming force and desire. Nothing else stands above it. It shines above the rest.

PRAYER: Thank you Lord that I am not alone in darkness. I ask for the light of Your glory to invade any dark space in my life. I desire to follow You alone, and to be led by Your light. Open my eyes to the reality of Your light in me.

YOU ARE
WITH US

AND DARKNESS MUST BOW

YOU ARE
WITH US

"And the light shines in the darkness, and the darkness did not comprehend it."
John 1:5 (NKJV)

I don't know any Christian who hasn't faced some form of resistance while pursuing the will of God. Opposition should not stop us as believers from moving forward. The truth is, darkness does not have the power to overcome light.

The word "comprehend" in the original language has to do with a dominating, a seizing, a pulling down, or holding under one's power.

It does not mean that darkness won't attempt to overcome, but it cannot seize light. Light always prevails. No matter what your situation looks like or feels like at the moment if you are a child of God and walking in the light, darkness does not have the ability to put out God's light. We must allow His to prevail and pull down the darkness.

1 John 5:4 (NKJV) says that "For whatever is born of God overcomes the world. And this is the victory that has overcome the world—our faith."

This scripture tells us that when we walk by faith, we enter right in the center of the ring where darkness is attempting to overthrow light. It is essential to understand that walking with God and stepping into faith does not mean that all problems will be removed from your life.

Paul says at one point he was "…struck down, but not destroyed" 2 Corinthians 4:9 (NKJV).

We are part of the incredible partnership with the Light of God. We always have the ability to get back up and to keep moving!

I remember an incident I had as a kid. I was running on a soccer field and unfortunately ran straight into the goal post! It knocked me flat on my back. I didn't even know what hit me or what had happened. For many people, this is what life feels like most of the time. When I ran full force into the post all I knew was that it hurt. Even though I was in pain, it wasn't long before I was back up on my feet and overcoming the soccer field!

PRAYER: Thank you Lord that You are the light, and that Your light is in me. I choose today to partner with You by seizing any darkness with Your light. I will not allow the cares of this world to keep me down. I will get back up, move forward and partner with You, Lord. Thank You that darkness has no chance when Your light shows up!

"Fear not, for I am with you: Be not dismayed, for I am your God. I will strengthen you, Yes, I will help you, I will uphold you with My righteous right hand." Isaiah 41:10 (NKJV)

I love this powerful promise – "Fear not for I am with you!" The reality of God's presence brings strength.

Often we build our perspectives around what I call "circumstantial theology." It is so important that we interpret our circumstances according to God's word and His ways. Sometimes we misappropriate God's word to fit our circumstance.

When Jesus started His public ministry He immediately taught that the Kingdom of God is present; it is here, and it is now. Jesus was not referring to a castle on a hill. He was talking about the reality of the reign of God.

In Matthew 6:9-10 (NASB) Jesus teaches us how to pray, "hallowed be Your name, Your kingdom come, Your will be done on earth as it is in Heaven." Jesus is stating here that the coming of the Kingdom would be the extent of God's rule, where His name is hallowed (honored as holy), and His will is done.

To receive Him is to receive His kingly rule, not only in your life and over your affairs, but also through your life, and by your service and love. "The kingdom of God is within you," Jesus said. Therefore, you get to enter into His strength. Fear runs, and strength rises as King Jesus is welcomed!

When I was a young boy, my parent's allowed my older brother and his friends to bring me along to the yogurt shop, which was just up the street from our house. I thought I was so cool. In my mind, I was invincible because I had my older brother with me. As we were

walking home, I was trying to act cool and started yelling out random, silly things. A guy driving down the street slammed on his breaks, got out of his car, and started yelling at me. At that moment I felt like a thousand-foot-tall giant because I knew my brother and all his friends were with me. The circumstance was against me, but the reality of presence caused my fear to scatter and strength to arise.

"The Lord is my light and my salvation; Whom shall I fear? The Lord is the strength of my life; Of whom shall I be afraid?" Psalm 27:1 (NKJV)

PRAYER: Father, I thank You for Your amazing presence! Open my eyes to the reality of who You are and the truth that You are with me. May fear vanish, and may Your strength arise in me. I trust in You, and I welcome you!

"And when the ark of the covenant of the Lord came into the camp, all Israel shouted so loudly that the earth shook. Now when the Philistines heard the noise of the shout, they said, "What does the sound of this great shout in the camp of the Hebrews mean?" Then they understood that the ark of the Lord had come into the camp." 1 Samuel 4:5-6 (NKJV)

Can you image a shout so loud that it shook the earth? Wow, what a fantastic sound it must have been when Israel shouted. I have been in sports arenas where the noise was so loud that you couldn't hear the person next to you talking. I'm not a big shouter, but there are times when there is just something worthy of a shout.

Several years ago my wife and I were on an airplane headed to Nashville. It happened to be Super Bowl Sunday, and everyone on the plane was watching. My wife is a big fan of one of the teams playing in the game. It was an absolute nail-biter. My wife's team was in the lead until they gave up an interception that cost them the game. The airplane resounded with gasps from the losing fans and shouts from the winning fans. I've never experienced anything quite like that on an airplane.

The word "shout" appears many times all throughout the Bible. It's mentioned so often because God is relaying an essential message to us. Power and authority are released upon the earth when we shout, and the result is victory. He wants us to shout His victory praise with our lives! It's time for the church to start shouting its declaration of God's goodness and power at a whole new level.

A shout can be a sign of victory, and it can also be a sign to the enemy. The Philistines asked, "What does the sound of this great shout in the camp of the Hebrews mean?" Why did they ask this? They asked because the atmosphere changed. As believers, we are

to alert the enemy that God is present. We are to shake the earth with the presence of God.

Shout to God with the voice of triumph! Psalm 47:1b (NKJV)

If we believe in the power of the presence of God, then we must bring His presence to our homes, our workplaces, and every place we go. Be an atmosphere changer! Pray daily that God's kingdom will come and His will be done on earth as it is in heaven. Remember, this is accomplished through you and me. This means that we must live our lives as a representation of God's kingdom on earth.

The sound that arose from Israel's camp declared the Lord's presence. Where God's presence is, there is life, liberty, and a sound of victory! We can shout God's goodness with our lives and make a statement to the world.

We have to let go of our worries about what other people think. God's presence gives us freedom. People of the world rely on circumstances to dictate their happiness. As Christians, our environment does not dictate us. We can have joy and victory even in tough times, knowing that God in us is higher than the enemy in the world.

PRAYER: Today I choose to declare the goodness of God. I won't let my circumstances dictate my environment. Lord, I ask for Your joy, knowing that whether my situations change or not, You are worthy of my praise. May the sound of my life to be an alarm to the enemy, and a sign to the world that God is present. I shout unto You God with shouts of victory!

Then he said to Him, "If Your Presence does not go with us, do not bring us up from here." Exodus 33:15 (NKJV)

It is easy for Christians to become familiar with their faith. Perhaps you grew up in a family focused on God and surrounded by a Christian community. Maybe there has never been a day in your life that you have not known Jesus as Lord and Savior. I understand this is not the case for many.

I've often wondered what would cause someone to make such a strong statement - If you don't go, I don't go! The reality of God with us dismantles fear and causes a courageous response within His people. This is exactly what happened to Moses. A face-to-face encounter with God Almighty changed the course of Moses's life. Just as this encounter between God and Moses changed everything for him, it will also change everything for you. The burning bush moment was the start of Moses' adventure with God!

God says to Moses, "take off your shoes" Exodus 3:5 (NKJV)

Very quickly Moses learns that he is in the presence of a holy God. Before anything else is said or done, Moses must come to a profound awareness of the holiness of God.

God says to him, "Do not come any closer. Take off your sandals, for the place where you are standing is holy ground." Exodus 3:5 (NKJV)

We also read that Moses hid his face because he was afraid to look at God.

Have you stopped lately to think about what it means to be in the presence of a holy God? It is so easy for us to treat God casually. Often, in our desire to spend time with God, we are distracted by

random thoughts and everything around us. Everything except God and His word becomes more important. Or we make commitments to God, but find that these commitments are quickly forgotten in the demands of the day. It takes self-discipline to focus your heart and full attention on the Lord.

Despite our tendency to wander, God has promised us that He is with us wherever we go. He is with us in the classroom, in the office, at home, on the road, and in the field. Remind yourself that you are serving a God who is Holy in all his ways, and who is present.

"Or do you not know that your body is the temple of the Holy Spirit who is in you, whom you have from God, and you are not your own?"
1 Corinthians 6:19 (NKJV)

If the reality of God's presence could cause a fearful man to move from fear to courage, how much more will He do for us? God is not just next to us, by us or our around us. He is in us! That's our daily truth.

PRAYER: Lord, let me be your servant today, in every word I speak, and in all that I do. I recognize that You are a holy God. I honor Your holiness and acknowledge my need for Your presence. Open my eyes to know that You are with me. Here I am Lord. Thank you that you are with me wherever I go. Give me courage today to move forward into new territory and Kingdom assignments. Amen!

"But you are a chosen generation, a royal priesthood, a holy nation, His own special people, that you may proclaim the praises of Him who called you out of darkness into His marvelous light." 1 Peter 2:9 (NKJV)

Everyone wants to be accepted. Many have had that moment in life where it's time to pick teams. Suddenly you're anxious over being the last one picked. Why? The answer is simple; everyone desires to feel valued and part of something. Most people spend their lives trying to earn acceptance.

In high school, I overheard many vain conversations of teenagers stressed out about their clothing and appearance. I even recall a young lady who didn't buy a pair of jeans simply because they weren't a certain brand. The need for approval and acceptance drives people in many areas of their lives. Often it is revealed by choices people make from clothing, cars, houses, and beyond. How many times have children (or adults for that matter) done something crazy, or even stupid, because they didn't want to be the outsider?

I was a basketball player growing up. It was one of my greatest passions. There wasn't a day that went by that I didn't shoot a ball or do something to increase my skill. I remember so vividly when I was chosen as a representative for the all-state team. The feeling of knowing that I was selected was incredible! It brought huge confidence to me.

You are chosen by God! He isn't just yours, but you are His. You don't have to strive to be a part. You don't have to earn it. He chose you. He loves you. He actually likes you! You can rest today in knowing that you are accepted.

Acceptance leads to confidence. Be confident today as a child of God knowing that you are accepted, and you are chosen. You are his!

PRAYER: Lord, I thank You for choosing me. You love me! You accept me! I choose today to lay down any form of striving to be accepted by You. I rest in the reality of Your love for me. I choose You. Help me to walk in confidence knowing that I am chosen. Amen!

"There is no fear in love; but perfect love casts out fear, because fear involves torment. But he who fears has not been made perfect in love."
1 John 4:18 (NKJV)

There are so many fears that people have. Fear of public speaking, fear of death, fear of lack, and the list goes on. The Bible tells us that perfect love casts out all fear. We should not minimize this life-changing verse to a mere quote. This powerful truth should become a daily consciousness of God's love.

Fear doesn't come from God. In fact, the Bible says, "God is love." (1 John 4:8b) So when you are afraid, remember that fear is not from God because there is no fear in love. God is love!

Awhile back I found myself in a place where I needed to cast out fear with perfect love. My wife and I were working on budgets for our ministry. We were thinking very minimal with a "just enough" mentality. We happened to be on an airplane while working on the budget. While I dictated my thoughts and ideas, Lydia transcribed them, interjecting her insights along the way. Suddenly, I heard the Lord speak to me about the numbers we came up with. Was what we had written down what we truly needed? I heard Him challenge me with this, "If that's what you write down, that's what I'll give you."

In that moment I realized I was operating in fear. We were playing it safe, and asking too little. The immediate awareness of His perfect love changed everything. I exposed fear with something greater – the perfect love of God. I told Lydia to stop typing and we began to think big, dream big, and ask big! You see, we knew God had given us a huge vision, yet we were afraid to ask for what we really needed. When I allowed the love of God to minister to me on that airplane, the budget went from minimal to something way bigger than us. Clearly, this could not be accomplished in my own strength.

Why is a personal revelation of God's perfect love so important? Because it's the key to living life free of fear. Fear has to be cast out. You cannot reason fear out. You cannot close your eyes and hope it goes away. How do you cast out darkness? You must command it, in the name of Jesus, to release its grip on you and go! By using the name of Jesus you expose fear to the Light. Darkness has no dominion in the light of Christ Jesus. Fear will leave when it has been exposed to something, or someone, greater and more powerful.

PRAYER: Lord, I thank You for Your perfect love. I cast down all fear right now in the powerful name of Jesus, and I expose fear to the greatness of who You are. I receive all of Your benefits and rest in Your peace. Help me Lord to live according to Your strength, and not my own. Amen!

"Brethren, I do not count myself to have apprehended; but one thing I do, forgetting those things which are behind and reaching forward to those things which are ahead, I press toward the goal for the prize of the upward call of God in Christ Jesus." Philippians 3:13-14 (NKJV)

We have all been at the place in life where there is a decision before us to move forward or turn back. It is tempting to glance back, or even to turn back to what once was, especially when the things in front of you are difficult. The reality is that sometimes turning back to the familiar appears easier than moving ahead into the unknown.

The children of Israel did this when things got difficult. They cried out to Moses grumbling saying "Let us select a leader and return to Egypt." Numbers 14:4 (NKJV)

When I was younger, I had the brilliant idea to go cliff diving with my friends. The hike to the top was great, but the moment of truth was when I was at the top looking down. All of the sudden I wasn't sure that this was such a good idea anymore. There were two ways down the cliff. One way was to hike back down. The other was to jump into the unknown trusting the water beneath me was deep enough. I decided to make the jump instead of turning back. I was able to experience something that I had never experienced before.

It is evident that turning back is not the way forward, but yet we still tend to look at what once was. Forward movement forces you to live by faith and not by sight, and the reason why going back seems so much easier. As the saying goes, "you have been there and done that!" It doesn't require faith to return to where you once were.

When I think of love as a banner, I think of a complete covering. God is love, and love casts out all fear. Being covered in His love means that we advance with a Godly perspective. We walk with confidence!

As sons and daughters of God, we are called to move forward in the will of God. Turning back isn't the way forward. It won't get you where you want or need, to go.

"Let all that you do be done with love." 1 Corinthians 16:14 (NKJV)

PRAYER: Thank you Lord that Your love is my banner. I take refuge under Your covering, and I choose to keep moving forward, and trusting in Your ways. I make a conscious decision to not look back, or turn back to my past, but to wholeheartedly trust You as my guide. Lord, thank You for the adventures that are awaiting me as I partner with Your Spirit, Your will, and Your ways!

"For the word of God is living and powerful, and sharper than any two-edged sword, piercing even to the division of soul and spirit, and of joints and marrow, and is a discerner of the thoughts and intents of the heart."
Hebrews 4:12 (NKJV)

What comes to mind when you read the word "discerner"? It may cause you to think of judgment, or someone who judges between good and evil. The language in this verse means to assess. The word of God reaches into the deepest places of our lives and assesses what is there. It searches all things, the good and the bad. It reveals the areas we are or are not aligned with His word. It exposes belief and unbelief. It assesses intentions.

The Word of God is the primary way we come to understand the truth about God. To stand upon His word means that you trust what His words are saying. This kind of trust results in strength and stability no matter what may come our way.

The word of God is not dead or ineffective. It has life-giving power! There is nothing more potent than a believer who chooses to stand upon the promises of God in the midst of difficulty, disappointment, and even times of despair. His Word is eternal and will not return void. It is more stable than anything you are looking for, sitting on, standing on, or feeling in this moment.

Most of the time we do not think about the ground beneath us. We just walk and continue taking steps. However, when the ground beneath is not stable, you are suddenly aware and more careful as you step. Years ago I was staying at a friends house in Los Angeles right after a major earthquake. They were still experiencing strong aftershocks, so everyone was a little on edge. It is incredible the scenarios our mind can conjure up when fear is present! That night I ended up on the bottom floor of their three-story house. I had seen enough

movies to believe that if another earthquake happened, I would be the first to be sucked up into the earth, or the house would fall on top of me. Both scenarios led to disaster! The truth is, I was paralyzed by fear of the earthquake.

We live in a world where the enemy paralyzes us with fear. There are horrific circumstances that arise daily across our nation, and the world, that cause deep fear in the hearts of men, women, and children. These fears bring division and confusion. People need something secure, safe and eternal to stand on. The Word of God is all those things and so much more! God has attached His presence and His power to His Word. We can stand on His Word with the confidence that it will never falter beneath our feet. His Word is, always, has been, and forever will be good! That's the kind of ground I choose to stand on.

PRAYER: Lord, I believe that Your Word has the power to defeat every adversary in my life! Today I stand upon Your living and powerful Word. Help me Lord to continue standing. I choose to be rooted in Your word, to speak Your word, and to release its power in my life. Amen!

"For though we walk in the flesh, we do not war according to the flesh. For the weapons of our warfare are not carnal but mighty in God for pulling down strongholds, casting down arguments and every high thing that exalts itself against the knowledge of God, bringing every thought into captivity to the obedience of Christ." 2 Corinthians 10:3-5 (NKJV)

God has invested His worth in each person He created. The adversary's primary means of sabotage is to break down our sense of worth and challenge our identity. God's Word says that the weapons of our warfare are mighty in God for pulling down strongholds.

What is a stronghold? A stronghold is a fortification, such as a fortified or strengthened city. However, there is another meaning of the word stronghold. It is also something that takes root in our lives as a pretense, in other words, a lie. It is something we believe, although it is just plain wrong.

A stronghold is a fortress or a prison. The walls are thick, cold, and lonely. You may have never before experienced what it is like in jail or stepped foot in a physical stronghold. But when the foundation we build our lives upon is lies and untruth, that is exactly what you are living in – a fortified stronghold, a prison, or a jail.

As a pastor, I have seen time and time again the destructive power of strongholds in people's lives. For many it starts with harsh words spoken over them by someone else, or even themselves. I've experienced this in my own life. Maybe you were told as a child that you couldn't sing, so you believed it. Maybe someone said something hurtful to you about your looks or your weight. Those words planted a seed, and little by little the seed grew up to be a fortress and a stronghold in your life. Sadly, many people live isolated within the walls of the internal fortresses they have built up through the years.

To witness a person's deliverance from this kind of bondage is truly miraculous! Suddenly the person can breathe in the fresh air of God, run freely, and enjoy every beautiful thing beyond the cold walls of their fortress. It is worthy of rejoicing over the freedom that comes when strongholds are torn down, and prisoners are set free.

The enemy has no right or power to enter our territory and build a stronghold unless we give him the permission to do so. A stronghold is an incorrect thinking pattern that has molded itself into our way of thinking. These strongholds can affect our feelings, how we respond to various situations in life, and they play a role in our spiritual freedom.

God wants you free today! Take authority over your life and step into freedom. Partner with the Holy Spirit and step out of the darkness and into the light and the fresh air. Breaking strongholds reveals the goodness and faithfulness of God.

PRAYER: Lord I thank You that I have freedom in you. Help me to break free from all fortified strongholds in my life. I declare Your word over every fortified fortress in my life, and I step into victory. Renew my mind today to believe Your Words, and tear down any lies that have become rooted in my life. I look to you and I trust Your word today. Thank you that I am victorious!

"I say then: Walk in the Spirit, and you shall not fulfill the lust of the flesh."
Galatians 5:16 (NKJV)

A lot of people ask God to give them the next steps, but don't always follow the path He reveals. The Scriptures teach us a much different way of doing things. Once you know God's will for your life, the next vital step is finding out how to follow and fulfill His will. It's not just about hitting a target. It's about the process of being led to the target.

Many believe that the end justifies the means. As long as they get from point "a" to point "b," it doesn't matter how they do it. That kind of logic leads to compromising lifestyles. People will do all kinds of crazy things to get where they want to go. They will lie, cheat, and even stab other people in the back so that they can "fulfill God's will" in their lives!

There is a right way and a wrong way to accomplish things. There is God's way, and there is the way of the flesh. The downfall of human nature is that we create our own will, timelines, and processes. However, if we allow the Spirit to lead us, our lives will flourish. Many people have misinterpreted what it means to walk with the Spirit. They are shocked when life is hard, and things don't come as easily as expected. Because of that mindset, many have left the fellowship of the body of Christ or even rejected God. I have learned, and history has taught us, that His Presence is enough. I would rather face difficulties and joys with Him, than have no difficulties without Him.

"For as many as are led by the Spirit of God, these are sons of God."
Romans 8:14 (NKJV)

We should continuously surrender and yield ourselves to the desires of the Spirit, whose leading is generally in direct warfare with our

flesh. Our surrender to the Spirit's leading is an act of the will, a choice we must make; it is saying yes to the Spirit's leading and no to the desires of the flesh.

I am not discounting the pull of sin, but Scripture is clear that if you walk by the Spirit you will not walk in the flesh. This truth could be stated many different ways. A few examples might include the following two sentences. If you are in the kitchen, you are not in the living room. If you are at the movies, you are not at the game. This is important because often times so much focus is placed upon sin and the act of sinning. The key take away from today's scripture is to stop focusing on the sin and start focusing on the Spirit! This is how we will begin to live and walk according to His Spirit.

The process of walking with God is exhilarating and so rewarding. He wants you to succeed more than you want yourself to succeed. He is for you and not against you. His plans for you are good!

PRAYER: Lord, I thank You today that I belong to You. What a gift you have given to me – the gift to walk and live empowered by your Holy Spirit! I submit myself to the leading of the Holy Spirit. I choose to not look for the easy route. I choose to look for You! I don't want to do anything on this path without Your partnership and guidance. I surrender to Your will for my life and trust You completely. Amen!

LET YOUR PRESENCE SHAKE THE GROUND

"The earth shook; The heavens also dropped rain at the presence of God; Sinai itself was moved at the presence of God, the God of Israel."
Psalm 68:8 (NKJV)

A few years ago my family and I were on vacation in Southern California. In the middle of the night, an earthquake hit. There was a loud rumble, and our condo began to shake. The shaking woke up my wife and me, but thankfully the kids slept right through it! The quake brought an awakening to us. We became aware of everything around us; the pictures hanging on the wall, the light fixtures and lamps, and anything that could break. As Lydia and I waited for the earthquake to die down, we recognized there was nothing we could do to stop it. We simply had to wait it out.

If God is shaking an area in your life, don't try to stop Him or rebuild yourself. Allow Him to restore only those things He wants to establish in your life. You are created for greatness! Remember, God shakes us so that anything not honoring or pleasing to Him will break off of us.

His shaking causes purification by exposing harmful things in our lives. His shaking also brings an awakening! If your affirmation, love, self-worth, joy, strength, and acceptance come from anyone but God, He will expose it and shake it! He does this so we will recognize that all these things can only be found in Him.

When His presence shakes and awakens, it brings an awareness of the greatness of God. The people of Israel were aware when the earth shook that someone bigger than them, their difficulties and their victories was present.

It's as simple as this - when God comes down, things will happen!

Whatever you are going through, whether a victory or difficulty, invite the mighty presence of God to invade your life!

PRAYER: Father I come to you, in the name of Jesus, and ask You to invade my life. I invite your shaking to expose any false beliefs and hindrances. I choose to recognize You as my only source! I trust in Your goodness and Your faithfulness. I welcome Your shaking and awakening power to inhabit my life. Amen!

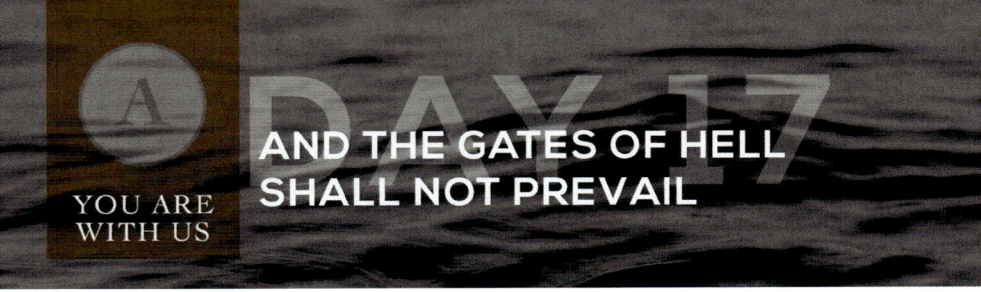

YOU ARE
WITH US

AND THE GATES OF HELL SHALL NOT PREVAIL

"And I also say to you that you are Peter, and on this rock I will build My church, and the gates of Hades shall not prevail against it."
Matthew 16:18 (NKJV)

One of my favorite spots in Israel is Caesarea Philippi. It is the location where Jesus had the famous conversation with Peter and the other disciples.

"When Jesus came into the region of Caesarea Philippi, He asked His disciples, saying, "Who do men say that I, the Son of Man, am?" So they said, "Some say John the Baptist, some Elijah, and others Jeremiah or one of the prophets." He said to them, "But who do you say that I am?" Simon Peter answered and said, "You are the Christ, the Son of the living God." Matthew 16:13-16 (NKJV)

Jesus took a seemingly vague question and made it personal. He asked His disciples, "Who do you say that I am?" Simon Peter answers Jesus, and in response to Peter Jesus says, "And I also say to you that you are Peter, and on this rock, I will build My church, and the gates of Hades shall not prevail against it." Matthew 16:18 (NKJV)

Before this event occurred, Jesus and His disciples were on their way to Jerusalem. However, Jesus led them on a much longer, more cumbersome route that ended up at a location far from Jerusalem. Why did Jesus do this? Because He had a compelling question, He wanted to ask, and a point He wanted to make. The people of that day believed the cave at Caesarea Philippi where this event took place was the gateway to hell, the literal satanic capital of the world. The evil sacrifices, idolatry, and satanic rituals that happened there were horrifying and sickening. In this demonic location, where so much evil took place, Jesus proclaimed that Satan and his kingdom will not prevail against the Kingdom of God and that He is the Christ, the Son of the Living God!

Thousands of years later, we are still answering this question: who do you say that He is? This question can only be answered individually. Your spouse, your parents, or your friends cannot answer it for you. You have to settle it for yourself. Our confidence still remains in the truth that Satan may come with force, yet he will not prevail!

PRAYER: Jesus, thank You for the assurance of Your victory against all the forces of hell and darkness. I ask You for courage and strength to attack the gates of the enemy with the truth of Your word. Today I settle in my heart, my mind, and my spirit that You are the Christ, the Son of the Living God. I surrender to You as my Lord and my God. Amen!

Jesus said to him, "I am the way, the truth, and the life. No one comes to the Father except through Me." John 14:6 (NKJV)

Take a moment and envision yourself in Jerusalem two thousand years ago. Pilgrims are pouring into the city from all directions. While this is a typical religious tradition, there is something different this year. The Jewish leaders are sick of this man named Jesus who is causing chaos wherever He goes, but whom so many are following. The Pharisees are desperate to arrest Him and regain control of the city.

The spiritual atmosphere is intense. Although the disciples don't fully understand what is happening, they sense the tension in the air. Later in the day Jesus will cry out to His Father in the garden of Gethsemane as the crushing pressure and realization of death comes upon Him. Judas will betray Him, and Peter will deny Him. The disciples are disturbed by all that is going on. They are ready to take things on in their earthly manner. Until the appointed time, Jesus continues to teach and give the disciples critical insights before His death.

Jesus urges them to trust in Him, and to lift their eyes to heaven. In the midst of the doubt, fear, and confusion, Thomas asks, "Lord; we don't know where You are going so how can we know the way?" Jesus responds, "I am the way, and the truth, and the life."

I remember a time I was in another country trying to figure out directions. I stood on the sidewalk staring at the sign trying to read a language I didn't understand. Confused and frustrated, I finally asked someone who spoke English to help me. The person kindly pointed out to me that written beneath the language I didn't understand were directions written in English. Needless to say, I felt pretty dumb upon the realization that the directions were right in front of me the entire time, and in a language I could read and understand. I was so

focused on trying to decipher the foreign language that I completely missed that my own language was on the sign, too.

If you want to live for God, Jesus is the way. If you desire to know the truth, Jesus is the truth. If you long to experience real life, Jesus is the life. Whether your life is filled with spiritual tension and difficulty, or you're experiencing peace and fulfillment, the truth remains that Jesus is the way, the truth, and the life.

Nobody wants just simply to live. People want to feel alive and experience life to the fullest. In this passage of scripture, Jesus is revealing to His disciples that not only does He give life, But He is also life! The only way to live the life we are designed by God to live is to come to Jesus and experience His fullness.

Today you have been given an opportunity to do just that. Just as I needed to open my eyes and look a little closer at the sign, perhaps you need to open your eyes and look to Jesus. Jesus is right in front of you pointing the way. If you need clarity and wisdom, Jesus is the truth. Don't settle for the counterfeit in your life. Come to Jesus, the one person who gave His life in order for you to have life, and live it abundantly!

PRAYER: Thank you Jesus that You are the way to eternal life and the answer to fulfillment and abundant living. Help me today Lord to recognize and let go of any counterfeit sources in my life. I make a conscious decision to cling to Your way, Your life, and Your truth in all areas of my life. Amen!

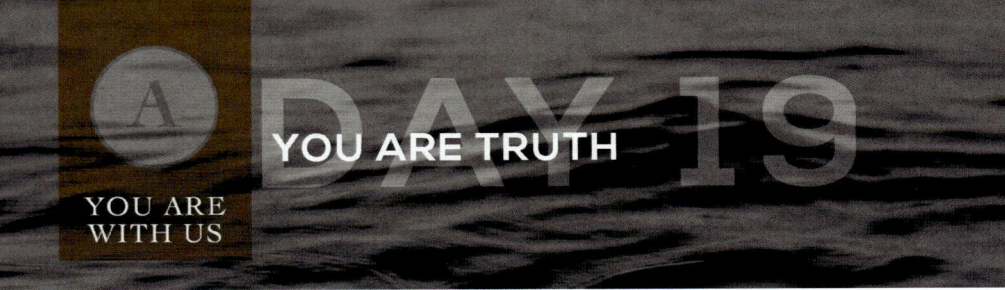

"Then Jesus said to those Jews who believed Him, "If you abide in My word, you are My disciples indeed. And you shall know the truth, and the truth shall make you free." John 8:31-32 (NKJV)

The world is full of false religions that claim to have prophets and leaders who speak on behalf of their god. However, Jesus declares something different about Himself. He doesn't just tell us the truth about God; He is the truth! Jesus is the express image of the Father.

Many have wondered and have asked, "what is God like?" The answer is Jesus. To see and know Jesus is to see and know God. Jesus shows a different way. He doesn't give a set of rules; He gives Himself. It is so important to remember that we don't read the Bible to gain understanding or learn truths about God. We read the Bible to encounter Jesus! When we encounter Him, we will know the truth, which is God.

I love reading the Bible! Countless times I have experienced the reality of the power of His Word as I've read the Scriptures. It's as if the words on the page jump out at me and grab my heart. I remember one time I was dealing with a difficult situation in the church I was pastoring. As I read Paul's writings, I felt like I was in a face-to-face conversation with Paul. It was as if he is sitting across the table encouraging me, challenging me, and exposing the lies of the enemy with the truth of his words. The Bible came alive to me at that moment and ministered to my most profound need. I was in tears as the living Word of God washed over me.

There is such a fierce spiritual battle for disciples of Jesus to have intimacy and fellowship with Him. Abiding in Jesus brings hope, strength, and freedom! As believers we don't just have access to words, we have the Word. We don't just have access to truths; we

have the Truth. Abiding in Him, who is the truth, sets us free. Truth is not an expression. Truth is a person, the person of Jesus Christ.

PRAYER: Lord, I chose today, and every day forward, to abide in You. Thank You that You abide in me. Help renew my mind to the realization that You don't just give truth, You are the truth. I ask for a fresh revelation of Your Word. I desire to know the truth and walk in Your freedom. Amen!

*"Behold, a virgin shall be with child, and shall bring forth a son, and they
shall call his name Emmanuel, which being interpreted is, God with us."*
Matthew 1:23 (KJV)

Emmanuel God is with us. God came to us. What a staggering thought that the God of the universe; the one who created the sun, the moon, the stars, and you and I, is with us! We are not alone. This truth is the essence of the Christian faith. Other religions teach a lifestyle of works; that you have to do certain things, and follow specific rules, to measure up and earn your way to Heaven. Christianity is based upon the redeeming love of Jesus Christ. The work that He accomplished for our freedom and healing at the Cross means that we do not have to live by works any longer. He measured up so that we can measure up!

It gets even better! He makes a way for us, but equally important, He Himself is with us. Being a Christian is not merely following a creed; it is having Christ Himself live in you and through you, giving you the strength to be the man or woman He has called you to be.

Awhile back I was on a plane heading home after a business trip. Some friends of mine were on the same flight. I had been feeling great and wasn't expecting what was about to happen to me. Suddenly I felt clammy, so I got up and headed towards the bathroom. However, I didn't make it. The next thing I remember was waking up with flight attendants standing over me. I had passed out in the middle of the airplane! The entire process was strange. I had no strength and didn't know what happened. Thankfully the flight was almost over, and we arrived soon after the incident. The paramedics met me at the gate. They evaluated me and cleared me after a few minutes. Before they let me go, they asked if I felt alright or if I needed further assistance. They offered to walk with me to the baggage claim area. I remember feeling such an enormous sense of peace and confidence knowing I was not alone. My friends who were on the flight with me never left

my side. They stuck with me the entire time. They carried my bags and were ready to help me with whatever I needed to get home.

The Bible does not say that we will have problem-free lives as followers of Christ. The Bible does teach that we never will be alone. And because of that, we don't have to be afraid.

We began today with the reality of "God with us" coming in the form of a child. Jesus' last words to His disciples were one final reminder that they did not need to fear because He will always be with them. The promise of God to be with us is the same promise today. We are not alone.

"Teaching them to observe all things whatsoever I have commanded you: and, lo, I am with you always, even unto the end of the world. Amen."
Matthew 28:20 (KJV)

PRAYER: Lord, I rest in the promise that I am not alone. I do not have to fear because You are with me. Because of this powerful truth, I chose to walk in the purpose and calling that You have for me with full confidence knowing that I am not walking alone. Amen!

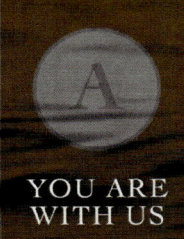
A 21

YOU ARE
WITH US

AT THE END OF IT ALL
WHEN OUR RACE IS RUN
WE WILL GIVE YOU THE CROWNS
YOU'VE ALREADY WON

"For we are His workmanship, created in Christ Jesus for good works,
which God prepared beforehand that we should walk in them."
Ephesians 2:10 (NKJV)

A disciple of Jesus Christ faces different challenges, one of them is living from a place of temporal perspective versus an eternal perspective. Everything in the world is so fast-paced. People want quick results. It is easy to misalign our priorities and lose sight of that which is truly important. We are called to be in the world, but not of the world. Ephesians 2:10 (NKJV) states that "God prepared good works for each one of us before we were even born so that we should walk in them." Pretty amazing isn't it?

All the stuff we love here on earth does not come with us to Heaven. Our cars, houses, clothes, phones, Starbucks, and the list goes on, stays here! The Bible talks about crowns in Heaven. Just the mention of this causes me to think from an eternal perspective. Heaven is where you will receive your ultimate reward. I won't go into a study on the crowns of Heaven. However, God clearly shows us that there is more to life than the earthly rewards you see and experience.

When you purpose to do the good works that He prepared for your life, you will do more for the Kingdom of God than you could ever imagine. Often in the mundane of everyday life, you don't realize the impact you have just by being obedient and faithful to God's Word and His call on your life. You will experience rewards on the earth, and in heaven! Imagine Jesus speaking these words to you at the end of your life, "well done good and faithful servant!" We don't have to live a life of striving. We merely have to walk in the steps prepared for us while on the earth. When we see Jesus face-to-face, we will enjoy heavenly crowns because of the steps we took.

Growing up my parents put sticky notes everywhere asking the question "Is this temporal or eternal?" Every time I read one of those notes it caused me to think about whether what seemed so important at the moment had an eternal perspective or temporal implications. What if our focus was not on collecting things on earth, but on our crown collection in Heaven?

My father-in-law passed away suddenly just four months before our wedding. The temporal reality was absolutely devastating. While paramedics and firefighters were still in the house, Lydia, my mother-in-law, my parents and I, stepped out onto the back porch. In our brokenness, we began to sing and worship the Lord. The invasion of the presence of God through worship immediately gave us an eternal perspective. At that moment, we knew that no matter what, we would get through the shock and the pain of such an unexpected loss.

A heavenly perspective keeps us grounded, rooted in truth, and gives us a healthy detachment of the things of this earth. It keeps us alert and focused. I encourage you to take a good look at your life and decide where your focus is.

PRAYER: Lord, I want my life, and all my earthly possessions, to reflect a life that is lived for You. Help me to live with the mindset of eternity. I desire to steward well and honor You with all that You have entrusted to me. Thank you for empowering me to do the works that You have prepared for me to walk in. Amen!

Made in the USA
Monee, IL
14 April 2021